# Rita Ann Higgins

## Pathogens Love A Patsy

### *Pandemic & Other Poems*

the arts council
an chomhairle ealaíon

funding literature
artscouncil.ie

Published in 2020 by
Salmon Poetry
Cliffs of Moher, County Clare, Ireland
Website: www.salmonpoetry.com
Email: info@salmonpoetry.com

ISBN 978-1-912561-90-2

Cover Artwork: *Sefa Ozel*
Cover Design & Typesetting: *Siobhán Hutson*

*Printed in Ireland by Sprint Print*

*Salmon Poetry gratefully acknowledges the support of*
*The Arts Council / An Chomhairle Ealaíon*

In memory of my sister

Mary Diviney

who died aged 67

on 16th February, 2020

In memory of my niece

Sharon Higgins

who died aged 50

on 15th February, 2020

# Acknowledgements

In 2020, many of the *Pandemic Poems* were broadcast on RTÉ Radio 1's *The Brendan O'Connor Show*. 'Scullery' was published in *The Irish Times,* edited by Gerry Smyth. The poems 'He Fell Through the Cracks', 'Beware the Geegaws' and 'The Spark', or versions of them, were published in *The Sunday Independent* in 2019. 'Mortal' appeared on the front page of *The Sunday Independent* on 10th November, 2019. Some of these poems were translated by Aleksandra Nikcevic-Batricevic and published in *Journal Fokalizator*, Podgorica, Montenegro, 2020.

'Proof' was first broadcast on BBC Radio 4 on 15th October, 2019 as part of the radio programme *My Modest Proposal*, produced for the BBC by Rockfinch Ltd. 'Homage' was released in the *Words Lightly Spoken* podcast series on 19th June, 2019. *Words Lightly Spoken* is also produced by Rockfinch Ltd. and the 2019 series was funded by the Arts Council of Ireland. 'Cavities' and 'Tooth and Nail' were published in *The Pickled Body,* issue 5.1, Winter 2019, edited by Patrick Chapman and Dimitra Xidous.

*Culture Unconfirmed,* a civic-led response to the Covid-19 crisis at the University of Liverpool, featured some of these poems in an audio presentation, curated by Professor Frank Shovlin, in May 2020.

On European Union Day, May 9th, 2020, the Greek Ministry of Culture accepted the proposal by Demitris Angelis, Director of the Athens World Poetry Festival, to show poets from all countries of the Union reading their work. Each country was represented by one poet. Rita Ann Higgins represented Ireland, reading her poem 'Cocoonery' on film.

The Hanna Greally poems (*Poems of Isolation*) were inspired by Greally's memoir *Birds' Nest Soup*, which documents her nearly two-decades-long incarceration in St. Loman's Psychiatric Hospital in Mullingar during the 1940s and 50s. Some of these poems are imagined and some are based on real events. *Birds' Nest Soup* was first published by Allen Figgis in 1971. Cork University Press republished the memoir in 2008 and it is still in print.

Special thanks to Patrick Chapman and to Jessie Lendennie and Siobhán Hutson of Salmon Poetry.

# Contents

# III
## *Poems Before Covid*

# I.
# *Pandemic Poems*

# Seal the Freezers

Try to come to terms with the fact
that flat 7-Up won't kill the virus.
Never mind sealing the borders,
seal the freezers that are chock-a-block
with white sliced pan.
The same tasty stalwart
when toasted and assaulted with loads of real butter
will end up filling you with more wind
than a thoroughbred at Cheltenham.
Tell the kids who are selling lines
to eff off, through the letterbox.
If you say it in Irish it takes the harm out of it.
Tell them you don't believe them about the first prize
'a part of a goat will be faxed to someone in Antarctica'.
Take positive action.
Enrol in a night class on hand washing.
Duration ten weeks. No refund.
But those carrying their own sink
will get priority.

# I Must Wash Down the Banister

I keep getting a reminder on my phone
that I'm running out of road.
Your iCloud is bursting lady, do something.
Will I get the extra storage space?
Or will I delete things?
Say if I delete videos of the kids and regret it.
I regret it already.
It's probably those audio books
but I can't bear to delete them.
*But you've listened to them all.*
What difference does that make?

Will my grandson be ok? the 'only child' one.
At least the other three have each other.
Will the only grandson be on his phone the whole time?
Will he miss his school friends so much it will damage him?
I don't want to pay the extra two ninety-nine a month.
It's wrecking my head. They are trying to catch me.
It was 99 cents first, next it will be five euro.
How do I log on to the iCloud?
I'll ring him, kids know all that stuff. He did.

Are the fourteen days up yet?
Can we go up to see the Ballybrit Three?
Is it fourteen days from day one
or fourteen days from the day I rang the doctor?
Will I wash the kitchen floor?
I must finish that book.
I should wash the kitchen floor.
I should wash my hands again.
I should freeze much more stuff.
Oh God we have no Lemsip.

Is he spending too much time in his room?
Is he lonely without his friends?
He says, I'm fine, we have loads of obair bhaile,
and we have interactive games.
Would you like to try writing a poem?
*No thanks Mamó you're grand.*
*I'm on a game with my friend,*
*talk soon, bye.*

Himself is downstairs I can hear him talking.
Did I hear you on WhatsApp to the boys?
Why didn't you call me I was just upstairs?
Were they Ok? Does JJ look tired?
She doesn't sleep well you know!
Is it fourteen days yet?
Did I hear you coughing a while ago?
Don't be going out the back without your jacket.

We watch the news.
You don't know how I can watch
four news channels at the same time.
I don't know either, I can't stop.
Can we go for a walk?
What's two metres in yards?
Where will we go, not the prom,
not the beach, there will be too many there.
We may as well stay in and watch Netflix or the news.
How many cases today?
It seems a lot.
I think it's in the air.
I must wash down that banister.
I know I've never done it before
but something is telling me to do it now.

# Cocoonery

There is no room for keeping
up or down a grudge
in these virus-packed days.
Let it go Minnie, let it go.
It's clear that fear
will make spies out of all of us.
Get in Minnie, get in.
A coffee and a bun today
will end up a funeral for one tomorrow.
Don't risk it Minnie, be afraid.

If your lungs fill with virus
it will turn to concrete
and breathe easy you will not.
You might be as fit as a falling fork
but stick to the rules Minnie, get in.

Resentments melt – grudges fall apart.
There is only room for looking differently
at every single thing.
Now is the new normal Minnie, latch onto it.
Isolate in our new police state.
Be one, not two.
Be three and the drones will see you
out walking your dog.

When you are stopped
be ready with your answers
Don't make jokes, this is no laughing matter.
Daily announcements – grim and grimmer.
Learn new words: patient zero,
super-spreader, pandemic, fomite,
social distancing, cocooning –

absolutely no mooning
on Prospect Hill or Gentian Hill.
Ignore run-along words like
alligators and ventilators.
Wear a face mask if you can.
Take only every second breath.
Stay at home, wash your hands.
Get intimate with your garden.
If you get symptoms –
start praying.

This is coronavirus
and we will beat it indoors
or it will beat you outdoors.
Leave resentments and old grudges
at the gate, they no longer carry weight.
Back away from that Tunnel of Fudge Minnie.
The stark warnings seek to terrify, they win.
Now is the new normal Minnie. Get in, get in.

# Even the Con Artist Weeds

Betty is coming to terms with nothing –
and nothing less than nothing equals something.
Gone are the heady days
when she would wolf-whistle at herself
for Tom's unfailing entertainment.

She knows for her to sidetrack
the many echoes, shades and visions of loneliness
that can ambush her in any coronavirus day –
she must act now.

The next ten days are crucial,
the voice on the radio says.
Adding fear to fear itself.
She draws the line at hugging herself –
for as long as she can memory up
the loving touch from the man
who held her nightly
for over fifty years, give or take,
she can brace herself for any calamity,
vortex or virus.

She remembers this
before she goes into the garden
and allows her fingers
to display a menacing mode
so far alien to her –
allowing her pull the heads off every weed
with sharp, aggressive snaps.

The way loss makes us evaluate
in insane ways is difficult to fathom.
She rattles out to no one in particular,
'If he can't be here neither can you.'
She continues the aggressve snapping.
The weeds pile high,
even the con artist weeds
like bindweed with its pink and violet trumpets,
flirting and choking
all at the same split second.
Not forgetting mister creeping buttercup
that has sly under-the-chin ways
of knowing if you like butter.
These weeds and their shameful inertia
come to terms with nothing
and nothing less than nothing equals something.
The next ten days are crucial,
the voice on the radio says.
Adding fear to fear itself.

# The Memo

Before the memo we were settling in
to mixed degrees of misery
and thinking that life could not get any worse,
after getting a real taste of
Ireland of the Welcomes
over the Easter weekend.
Spy culture was the vulture
you didn't want to meet
and you decked out
in puce camouflage lycra
trying to break into
your own mobile home.

Now we foment rebellion
from our sitting rooms nightly –
more crisps more coke.
The dirty memo that riled us
goes ludicrously close to jibber jabber.
It's not the memo that you think it is,
it's the other one,
the less important one
that got thrown in the 'who cares' drawer
that categorised our elders as follows:

They are clean if they are virus-free.
They are dirty if they are suspected of having the virus.
They are dirtiest if they are a Covid-19er.
We are in the tumble dryer
where they can't hear our footfall.
Every eye is a spy.

There is no peak to be flattened.
We sat on the peak weeks ago
while other countries sat on the fence –
this is not a time for triumphalism.
Think microwave think second wave
we are 56 days in.
We are taking umbrage.

It's as if elders in nursing homes
were numbers to be counted –
but do they really count
when push comes to shove?
Don't mention shove to me
or an older memo comes to mind
the one that called
longtime hospital patients trespassers.
That memo gave 'minimum force rights'
to overworked nurses
to get them – trespassers – out of that bed.
Bed blockers was another barb floated.

Is a leaked memo just a leaked memo
or a microcosm for something else?
Who knows? Ireland's call took an awful fall
and it was ding-dong doable.
It was all me love you long time,
me want you, me don't want you.
We hum in riddles, we blather in bile.
We take umbrage.
But the memo takes more.

Dirty memos do what dirty memos do best –
they leak out. And free postcards sneak in.
Is it me or are those postcards hideous?
The aesthetic is pathetic, ergo the cards are free.
Still in the tumble dryer and my hair is like straw.

Nursing homes and long-term care facilities
were second thoughts,
and maybe third thoughts,
when the virus was well under the table.
We took umbrage
but the memo took more.

# Pathogens Love a Patsy

Don't be getting ahead
of where we need to be.
Where we need to be
is not where we are.
We are waiting for the phases.
Phase one is coming soon but not soon enough.
The fifth of never, never came, and never will.
The 18th of May is a red-carpet speech away.
Wait and seek, hide and find.
Stay well behind.

Listen to the experts if you like.
You don't have to believe them, but be kind.
The coronavirus clichés are clocking up.
We don't want the cure to be worse than the disease.
We are not reaching our milestones
but our liver stones are as big as beach balls;
don't mention beach to me.

Operation Fanacht
won't let you breach the beach
or drink the bleach this bank holiday.
Operation Fanacht will be like Frances Thomson's
Hound of Heaven — it *will chase you
down the nights and down the days.*
Except when the text says:
Your fry is on the table loveen —
you'll hear the sirens then.
Or when another Garda says,
come on now Jimmy for a game-a-spot;
let them breach the beach
and drink all the bleach they want Jimmy.

We all know there's a virus in the village
and it's coming home to roost.
We are doing our Trojan best.
The drones are coming
and taking high-res photos of your car.
They can see all those choc-ice wrappers
under the seats. Trust no one.
Is that a mobile home parked outside your car
or are you just happy to see me?

Melania Murphy
is shredding the net curtains
with her teeth, watching those day-trippers
galloping over the lacuna,
and she boxed in since God knows when.
Operation Fanacht has no power over the lacuna.
All Melania Murphy has to look forward to
is the filth proffered in the multiple ads
she sees nightly for *Normal People*.

Operation Fanacht
won't let you breach the beach,
drink the bleach or eat your young.
The biggest devils
are the smallest airborne aerosols
lurking in the aisles of supermarkets.
Waiting for you to breathe them out
or your neighbour to breath them in.
Pathogens love a patsy, move on.
Mask up, mask often, wash them hands.

Don't be an ass in the aisle,
never mind the minutiae
on the yoghurt label, move on.
Get fresh air into your lungs.
Hug your cat or your dog,
take affection where you can.
Pathogens love a patsy, move on.

# Knee Deep in NPHET

The overgrown grass
in the space in front of the houses
is making me feel abandoned and half-crazed.
In the past eyebrows were raised
at wans out cleaning the estate
and rolling in the clover with hedge clippers
and makeshift grass pans.
Doing the Corpo out of a job was the
raised-eyebrow interpretation.
Now I want to do the mowing myself.
I'm craving a Stiga tractor mower –
a ride-on with room for a pet weasel.

I'm trying to get the hairdresser to do a house call
and take this greyness from my life.
The rainy-day money is on the table, she's nearly there,
I might have to throw himself in to seal the deal.
On top of that I'm knee deep in NPHET updates.

The four humors sneak up on us
in a time of Covid-19
and cause much chaos.
Your yellow and black bile
is never a good chat-up line.
I heard leeches are great for that.
Not everyone loves a leech
but James Joyce did
and he slapped them round his eyes
to nobble the gallop of his blindness.
It never worked, sadly.

Nowadays we need to look on the plusses.
Every household in this sprawling
working class estate is ecstatic

that golf and tennis will be allowed
in the next stage of opening up essential services.
Thanks for thinking of us NPHET.
NPHET really matters but NPHET doesn't rhyme.

When the 'allowed' are not out playing golf
they are wiping the sweat off their tennis balls.
Sweaty tennis balls can harbor virus,
but don't you worry, most tennis clubs
will supply fully disinfected ball baths.
Stand-alone or double ball baths,
depending on your membership tier.
You can dip, walk and wipe
if you are a Gold Circle member.
On the other hand, you can sit,
bathe and bounce your tennis balls
before a second immersion –
if you are a Platinum member.
Membership tier is everything.

Working class love a remedy,
working class love a rhyme.
We might hold out for the Remdesiver.
If there is any left over.
Thanks for giving us back
the golf and the tennis NPHET.
It was missing from our lives.
NPHET rhymes with nothing
only means that NPHET doesn't rhyme;
it never means NPHET doesn't matter.
NPHET matters all the time.

(NPHET: National Public Health Emergency Team)

# A Beacon from Mars

Phase one of easing the restrictions
is a bit frightening.
Find four people and talk to them
in the middle of the road.
You don't have to know them.
In fact, it's better if they are strangers.
Don't bring them into your house.
Don't roll around on the chrysanthemums
in the garden centre.
People will think you are weird.

Be totally confused
about homeware and hardware.
If you are a hardware shop
and you have homeware, it's win-win.
On the other hand,
if you are a homeware with no hardware
then look in the window
of the hardware shop and cry.
Face covering can be anything
from a dish cloth to a duvet.
Don't say mask, never say mask.

Don't be tempted to run
into other shops without thinking.
A sugar rush today without your balaclava
or your blanket could mean
a stay in ICU tomorrow, don't do it.

The Leaving Cert is cancelled,
calculated grading is in.
Teachers are under pressure.

All contact is forbidden.
If you happen to see your teacher on the prom
don't say, Dia dhuit a Mhúinteoir.
That could be viewed as canvassing.
Just keep looking into your shoes,
and mind the bollards.
The teacher tension was knitted as tight
as fishing gut covering a gully –
student tension was tighter.

Outside the chaos, is more chaos.
Mammograms are not happening;
neither are cervical checks.
Childcare, who-care, why-care, no-care.

But there is a ray of hope.
It might be safe to let
the children back to school soon –
then again it might not.

The meat factory workers
stand shoulder to shoulder.
Where do we stand?
As long as our sirloin is on the plate
do we really care?
More onions there love.

The tourists will be coming soon
through our common twilight zone,
bringing the virus in their pockets.
The advice we were given in March
is flying in the face of our isolating sacrifices.

The road-map to recovery is flashing
like a beacon from Mars.
Contact tracing is more myth than menace:
*'the systems don't talk to each other'.*
The graph says we think it's over.
It's not over till the coronavirus ends —
and the virus has more heads than the Hydra.
Be careful with the Hydra,
when one head dies two heads live.

# Life Will Be Different

We are tired of pandemic-isms
that were banged around
like bin lids during the troubles.
Who are we now when we are not using new words
that are pandemic-steeped-and-pickled.
It has been every waking minute
a pandemic zone and we are sick of it.
Antibody talk and cures that are not cures at all.
Walk three times sideways
under your shadow, for this to work
align yourself and your shadow.
Do this for *two hours and two hours only.*

Other aforementioned cures
involve heavy-duty bleach.
Don't do it, your insides won't *hold.*
And you will be *slouching* to the vet,
your eyes rolling down your face
looking for their sockets.
We have become pandemic experts
and pandemic poets.

We are mourning our lives before this.
When we took for granted simple things
like *free money*, like parking at the beach
before the appearance of the orange cone,
which has now taken on a sinister hue.
Look around before you spin
that cone into infinity.
The pandemic police
are hiding in the very long grass.

We will do old things again,
like walk into TK Maxx
and fit on a Prussian-blue blouse
that won't fit, and those Salsa Jeans
that look at you as if to say,
who are you kidding?
We fed that virus for months
and now the muffin-top repels us.
We will be slim again
and the virus will be gone.
But not if we are to believe
some nay-sayers
who say it will be with us
all the Christmases of our lives.

Someday we will sit in a pub
with our hair coloured and coiffed.
Laughter will be absent
from the space between us.
That expanse will make us cautious –
and awkward.

We will wave to people across the street
but gone are the whispering sessions,
where you'd gasp on hearing some juicy gossip,
or insider information about white collar coke-heads
watching porn for forty-eight hours
on a bank holiday weekend.
A pirated clip from *Normal People* on a loop
is a purported favourite.
From now on when you meet old friends
you will just wave and life will be different.

The day I long for most
is the day I can pop into Penney's
for the cheap knickers and cosy pyjamas.
I might throw in a pair of slippers,
with the *free money*.
When that day comes
I will make an altar in the garden,
I will burn incense sticks – myrrh, ylang ylang.
I will pay homage.
I will howl for all I am worth.

# A Few Morsels for the Mortals

In Greek mythology the phoenix
rises out of the ashes to live another day.
In homegrown mythology the phoenix
was only an aul peacock in disguise.

See no virus, hear no virus.
Ergo, where the virus?
Not in P. Park on a sunny Sunday in May
Where P-I-C still means Person in Charge.
Let's picnic on higher ground
with our 'tinnies' and our shirts off.
Let's stand and clink.
It's all about the optics.

Who could blame US for seeking
a bit of boy-candy!
Truth is we didn't seek it,
it was foisted upon us.
That said it allowed us to take our eyes off the virus
and let them fall on the pecs and the hips,
the picnic basket and the ball.

With six-packs of confusion
and more mixed messages
than you'd find in a Matt Damon plastic bag.
We the pandemic schmucks yawned
and looked askance at our forfeit.

We demonised our little vectors
who were not vectors at all
and deprived them of hugs for months on end.
We can hug them now and check them
for headlice and ringworm at the same time.
Maith sibh, NPHET.

We sent our parents and grandparents to the abyss,
dropped a bag on their porch and ran.
No, it wasn't a Matt Damon bag,
it was a bag full of trans fats and treacle.
Giving them diverticulitis on top of
post-traumatic stress disorder.

But we did keep them from larking in the Park
and two-metres-apart, when a metre matters,
in the interest of something or other.

This is Gull Park not P. Park
Here the raucous sounds from gulls and crows
are pushing up the serial killer proclivity
we didn't know we had.
Prompting us to hiss out the incantation.
*Give us a metre and we'll take a mile,*
*and what do we have to do*
*to get a few cans around here?*

We are regular mortals after all,
no super-pecs of any kind.
No mythology to magic away
our gripes and groans,
not least while there is a pandemic
flapping around our four green fields.

We'll take some treats from a safe distance,
a few morsels for the mortals.
Our reckoning which is skewed
(by more than two metres in a crooked mile)
has some innate sensibility
which coaxes us to look up to the P-I-C.
We don't judge the pecs, hips, socks,
the picnic basket or the ball.
All we really desire is the phoenix to rise
and the peacock to fall.

# Against Forgetting

We are the guarded townies
of our own lost lives,
coming out into the world again
like fledglings with medical degrees.
We met the nice and the ne'er-do-wells
in the underworld.

To get where we are,
some of us had to visit the dystopian
Covid-19 test site at Galway airport and elsewhere.
When the testers wave (a slow wave)
you see six eyes as you drive past.
You will never know if they are smiling.

It's June and every day is a Sunday.
It's a long time since Cheltenham.
There is a sinkhole in the public finances,
they will end up taxing our toenails.
Hippie crack is on the rise, so are pods.
Our boy children look like girl children
with their long hair. There is no gender.
Don't mention school openings.
We are in-between
the river Styx and Hades.
The underworld has no light
and precious little small talk.
We are guarded and everyone is a burglar –
they are going to steal our garden hose.
Bring in that scooter for the love of Mike.

We are a heartbeat behind
the rest of the world,
and that heartbeat has a slow puncture.
Thank God *Normal People* is over.

In the 'how can we forget' place
there is a top ten.
How can we forget the restaurant owner
who said the Covid-19 payment
was like winning the lotto.
The same owner deducts coins
for coffee and chips from staff,
whether they sup or not.
It's called tough-luck lunch.
We remember.

I wear a mask and gloves in the supermarket.
My eyes light up when I meet another
mask-and-glover.
They are few and far between.
We are moving out but pulling back.
The louder they speak the more I fear them.
They too could be smiling.

From the top ten list comes another memory.
Remember the direct provision center
where the boiler didn't work
and strangers had to share a room
in a time of coronavirus.

A minister took out a full-page ad
in a Kerry newspaper
to apologise to the people of the town
for opening a direct provision centre
and not kowtowing first.
The people with the two-bar heaters
were nowhere to be found
in the full-page apology.
How could we forget?

We are ten weeks in —
we are edging into phase two,
which is phase one dickied up.
We are a heartbeat behind
the rest of the world.
We are getting older,
other news is occupying us.
Minneapolis.
The Trudeau pause,
Lafayette park.
George Floyd,
manacled,
asphyxiated,
deceased.
We remember.

# Keep the R-Rate Down

Keep the R-rate down.
In Orwell's *Animal Farm*
the rats were the pits
and blasted to outer Siberia.
Then after a while
they were brought in from the cold.
Ratfink, a right rat, ratbag,
it was rat this and rat that,
ratatouille and rat-a-tat-tat
and then there was a vote
and the rats were allowed in.
Respect Ro' was the cat-call
or the rat-call.

Their isolation was over.
Soon they would be
in decision-making positions.
But what ratbag wants to ratify
or rattle or indeed revolt?
The vote changes everything
or the vote changes nothing.
Vote early, vote rat.

While we humans were agonising
about the other R-Number
the rats started coming out of the sewers.
Horse-like rats, rats with saddles,
rats with sidekicks.
They moved from broken drains
to broken veins. Rats with masks.
They scuttled in the coal bunker,
rattling around rat-arsed.
They swaggered in the streets,
they ponced in the park.

Suddenly they were everywhere,
ubiquitous rats. Rats with hats.
Rats with bicycles. Rats with tricycles.
Suited rats, booted rats.
Rats with roles, rats up poles.
They wanted big jobs,
they wanted to govern.
Some rats would ratchet up a row
and say, shut your rat-trap
or go back to your rat-hole, ratfink.
Others would rattle on ad nauseam
about the rat-race,
speechifying but saying rat-all-at-all.

# Nothing is Random

We are edging closer to June 29th.
The roadmap to recovery
is flapping like a saloon door in *High Noon*.
Our good behaviour
has given us some reprieve.
Phase Three is imminent.

Something tells us we should be more upbeat;
we are, after all, winners of sorts.
Trust is hard won in this new place.
The out-the-other-end place,
the still-above-ground place.
We keep a gimlet eye out
for anything strange.
We rarely see the plank in our own eye
yet we spotify the speck in others.
We need to work on that.
Speck-spotting can lead
to other righteous behaviours –
like mask-shaming.

The masses will wear masks.
Sooner rather than never.
The fear is, we can't wear a mask
and wash our hands at the same time.
Trust us, we can do it!

Traffic is increasing, so are bad drivers.
Mister Empty is everywhere.
The soul of the city went on sabbatical,
leaving us bereft.
The fifty number is flashing subliminally.
We should be having a coming out party,
but feeling the joy feels weird.

We are still in vacuous times.
The space between us, ourselves and you,
is stretching like a clown's waistband.
Inwardly we summon cacophony and clack –
Outwardly we look stunned.

Our inner tumbleweed is giving us away.
For God's sake don't rattle us,
our borborigmus will be heard in Rome.
We are not sure how to behave.
Its random, isn't it,
this ephemeral thing, this uncertainty?
It won't have your back.
It will be at the roundabout
when you're at the park.
It's like the virus, we can't trust it.

We have changed over these months.
It's easier to tell ourselves we're the same.
So much to process
and thinking differently is fatiguing.
We never got that memo,
or the one about mortality either.
You wonder why the person in the mirror
with the broken capillaries
is in your house, wearing your clothes.

We are edging closer to the 29th.
Shops and gyms and the devil-knows-what.
Mass-goers can attend, but fifty only.
*Remember that day God said to Abraham,*
*if you only find fifty*
*righteous people in Sodom and Gomorrah*
*I will not destroy both cities.*
Maybe this is where the fifty came from.

Some sceptics say the fifty was plucked
out of the dark sanctum
and thrown randomly into the pot.
The inner voice on the full licence
tells you, nothing is random,
everything is weighed out –
measure for measure –
*and whatever measure you measure,*
*it will be measured to you.* (Matthew 7:2)

II.

# Poems of Isolation

# I'm Hanna Greally

*(and I want to go home)*

### 1.

All you needed to get out of here
was a letter.
It could be three lines
or five lines or six lines.
It didn't have to be
from a near relative
but if it was from
a loving mother,
then surely it would
carry you across the Shannon!

### 2.

The letter had only to be
from a responsible person.
A person who didn't hear voices
or have vivid dreams.
A person who didn't rub shite
in their hair.
Just a regular, boring person –
with a box room going-a-begging
if you didn't have a home to go to.
An address was the thing.

3.

It didn't matter
how many layers of clothes
you had on in the big house.
I liked a layer, I liked to hide my shape
even though a man once said to me
I was Voluptua, whatever that meant.
No matter how many layers you had on
the superintendent could always
see through you, right through to your tired sinews –
and like a big tell-tattler
he'd tell your mother –
*I think she needs more rest.*


4.

Mother would have her ammunition then
and she'd flaunt it like a tablecloth from the *Titanic*.
Oh, I'd love to take you home loveen
but the superintendent said
you needed more rest.
I always pushed the anger down
when she said that, way down into my shoes.
In truth I was having a Black & Decker moment
when she said that about rest.
She loved the word rest,
she'd throw it at me in the most loving way.
You need more rest, Pet.
Pet got me every time
and I'd yawn like a lunatic
and say, you are always right, Mother,
and my resting head
would weight her shoulder down and down.

5.

Daddy died when I was five.
I was told that he was kind and he loved me.
He sang lullabies to me. More of it.
The lullabies get flung at ya,
you can't remember so what can you say.
You are giving memories to have —
here are the memories I've chosen for you,
put them in a sandwich and bite down.
I have to think of how hard it was for Mother.
She told me Noreen's twins had a birthday Sunday.
She didn't know what age they were but she thinks four.
Noreen is our lovely neighbour.
One night I dreamt Noreen was my mother.
I never told Mother though.
You can only have one mother.
We don't pick them but our mother is our mother.


6.

On the next visit
I said to Mother,
you can search me like a sieve
but you won't find any trace of a yawn.
Go on, look inside the intima, Mother.
What do you see?
Nothing but a well-rested
nineteen-year-old, gagging to go home.

7.

We didn't even know that Ginger was pregnant.
There was no mistaking those screams
on the 30th of February, 1945.
That baby was catapulted off for adoption,
by a nun with a nose like a pencil –
before we had a chance to say,
was it a boy or a child?


8.

You'd never know
if anyone was pregnant here.
Our clothes are like shrouds,
dull and donn and big as boats.
We'd look perfectly at home in coffins.
In fact, sometimes I'd nearly go as far
as to say, you'd look great in a coffin, Sister.
We'd laugh at that. We'd laugh at anything.
Laughing is better than waiting.


9.

The girls are on to me about the dance –
skittish and childlike – they never stop.
Swopping hair bands and glittery slides,
all the while whooping like swans.
Goretti gave me her best red shoes.
I say to them, woah there, fillies.
It's all well and good for ye
getting yourselves up to ninety-eight
but I'll hardly be here.
I'll be long claimed out
by the time the next fox trots out.

10.

At the next visit
I said, Mother get off the cross
and put that cranky face in your pocket.
Well that's what the inner waif in me was saying.
It wasn't like a proper escape attempt, I told her.
I just said to myself,
here you are, young girl raking these leaves,
have a look outside that old gate.
It was a bit of an Adam and the apple scenario –
but there was no one here wearing a fig leaf, believe me.
I kept raking the leaves and smiling to myself
then I said to myself by way of internal dialogue,
I'll have a quick look outside.
I love a bit of internal dialogue.
I'd love to see a man wearing a fig leaf.
I looked outside
and saw the thistles.
The nurse saw me looking.
The thistles saw nothing.


11.

Trisha gets sad at this time of year.
The guard came to our house, she said
I would never hurt baby Thomas and I never did.
We should have left you in the laundry, her mother said.
I wish they had, Trisha said.
Pluck the memories you have Trisha, the good memories,
and play them over and over.
Trisha said there were finger memories and toe memories
and button-nose memories. Even though I only had him
for three days I can still recall the feelings around him.
He was swaddled in unconditional love, Thomas was.

12.

My appetite was poor because it was ages since our last visit.
Are you ok? I worry about you, Mother.
The insulin injections make me vomit like anything, Mother.
Now, now, Pet. The course will be over soon.
I was speaking to the wind and the trees.
No one was listening. Mother was whirly-gigging.
Her scarf sliding off the chair.
She was up, she was down.
Her powder fell, it went all over the place.
Oh, look at the time, the visit is nearly over.
My lift, my lift is waiting.
Mind yourself, Pet, until our next visit.


13.

The pall that falls over that dance floor
when we are shuffling out.
It's like a tattered overcoat.
It hangs but it doesn't.
It falls but it floats.
It has little comfort
but lots of draughts.
Then for a splintered second
our loneliness is complete.
The dancehall door is opened wide.
Men to the left,
women to the right.

14.

Who in their right minds would ask for
insulin shock treatments?
Mother replied, wearing her uppity voice,
even though she no longer owned a hundred acres,
and her furs were long gone with the good china.
She was lucky to have a brown sauce bottle
to drink her tea out of now.
No insurance when Daddy died made a pauper out of her.
It's because you are under twenty-one, Pet.
If I didn't sign for it, Pet, how would you get it?
I had the devil's own time with the internal voice just then,
it kept calling her the 'C' word.
It kept saying, *you chameleon, you big ugly chameleon.*
Only calling anyone ugly was a sin.


15.

I'm here Mother because you and this fooleen in front of you
aka me, agreed that I needed a rest, your favorite word.
Now I'm shot to shit with these injections.
Ready. Aim. Fire. Maim Hanna with your ire.
Every morning after the treatment
some benevolent with a grin as broad as China
planks a big bowl of glucose
in front of me as a chaser.
I'm supposed to applaud that tit-wit.
She stands in front of me like seven fools.
Stomach that, would you!

### 16.

Language, Pet, please. Is that any way for a young lady to talk?
You tried to escape, Pet, and acts like that have ramifications.
Internal name-caller please stop with the name-calling.
*Dog-shite-face, reptile relic, C is for cock-a-doodle-do.*
Ok I said, looking straight into her pupils,
which seem to me to be spinning around.
I'll finish the course, Mother —
then can I go home?


### 17.

I loved Mother and hated to disappoint her.
I can't speak for the wayward waif inside me
who wanted occasionally to remove her toenails
with a Black & Decker —
especially when she praised all the staff in here.
She wasn't here in the middle of the night
when nurse Nasty Nora
would put the lights on for two hours
just for badness.
The same nurse was left at the altar.
Now wasn't he the lucky fucker?
He'd never get a wink of sleep
with that cracked bitch around him.
He was terrified of her,
always touching his privates.

## 18.

My twenty-first birthday didn't hang about.
I nearly missed it waiting to be claimed out.
Waiting is for fools and sailors.
You'd never see an albatross waiting.
They fly in their sleep,
that's how little they wait.
Another thing about the albatross,
they don't flap. We flap all day,
where does it get us?
We should be more like the albatross.

## 19.

This was society's cesspool,
society's shite bucket.
Craturs were just left here and not claimed.
Thousands of them.
Calculating relatives often signed people in
and just left them here.
Poor devils with leaky brains and acres galore.
Most important of all, it was free.
Three hots a day and a cot.
A prison by any other name.
Only, when you are sentenced in a court
you get a release date.
I'm always hopeful that's me, Hanna Hopeful.
More birthdays came and went.
I was embarrassed by my birthday.
I never told anyone when it was.
It meant I was still here.
I've always hated that
happy birthday song, so juvenile.
So fucking EMPTY.

## 20.

If Nasty Nora saw you talking casually
with one of the men,
from any of the many shops around here
in this crazy little village, only it was not so little,
it housed three thousand patients.
It had tuck shops, hardware shops, carpentry shops.
More like sheds but you could get stuff.
She'd haul you into her office and make something
dirty out of it. *Don't tell me you were*
*talking to him about making you a coffin, Hanna Hopeful.*
*Were you asking that carpenter to lie in the field with you?*
*You dirty little witch, I'm on to you.*


## 21.

Treatments meandered in like arrogant relatives.
Salts instead of porridge,
sedatives if you leave your beak open.
Keep your lips pursed at all times.
Liquid paraffin for supper.
We didn't know how good we had it
until they tried to light us up.
That Lecky therapy would whip us into shape.
You'd be compliant after that sizzler.
Hisssss. Bite down girl, bite down, Hanna.
Shake, rattle and roll.
*Flipsake Hanna, you're getting sick on your nightie.*
*Have you no shame.*
*The nightie your mother bought you*
*for that birthday, which one was it? Tick tock.*
*Is that blood. Have you your friend, Hanna?*
*Why didn't you tell us?*

### 22.

Every time I farted crooked
it was a setback.
We were watched like you'd watch bacteria.
You would never see them
but they had it all written down about you.
Hanna did this, Hanna did that, Hanna tried to escape again.
More rest for Hanna, more rest. More Lecky.
Make her sizzle. It quieted her the last time.
No one ever said pay Hanna for all that work
she does in the laundry. Pay Hanna nothing.
Hanna is an unpaid slave.
But she gets the bishop's frocks good and stiff
with two spoons of starch in the wash.
The stiffer they are the better the bishop likes it.

### 23.

The girls kept me going, mostly.
They knew about the many ways to be lonely —
in one day, in one hour, in one minute.
They knew the colour and smell of loneliness.
We would never show the note-takers
our true selves, our true feelings.
The observers saw what they wanted to see.
They reported the mundane stuff.
*She was seen looking closely at that window.*
*She was seen looking closely at the delivery van.*
They saw nothing that represented the woman in us.
They never looked in our eyes.
They never saw the lonely in our eyes.
They never saw the person.
Or if they did it frightened them
into their silliness.

She was seen looking at the torn chicken-wire fence.
She was seen looking at the hole in the roof in the woodshed.
She was seen eating all her porridge.
She was seen leaving half her porridge.
We were seen but they were blind.
They never saw the human in us.
The person they saw had no dignity.
They could treat us like prisoners with no hope.
On top of that there was a distance thing,
you'd swear we had T.B.
They'd stick to the side of the wall
when you were passing.
You were an untouchable,
unless they were inflicting pain.
Then you were putty in their hands.


     24.

The girls would die of embarrassment
when I'd start on about the fact I'd be going home soon.
They'd change the subject,
they'd talk about Goretti's husband.
He signs her in, he signs her out. Yada, yada.
They were hurt for me too. I could see it in their eyes,
they were like the Madonna looking off to the side,
streaks of pity pulling down her face.

25.

Mother's visits were often strange.
She was caught in the vortex,
always whirly-gigging around.
*Will you stand the fuck still, Mother?*
*Or I'll pull your teeth out with my Black & Decker!*
I'm getting a lift off Kelly's I can't keep them waiting.
I understand, Mother.
My best friend died.
I understand, Mother.
The cat got lockjaw and now he has a strep throat.
I understand, Mother.
My cardplaying friend has an unmentionable down there –
I understand, Mother.
Money is tight, I had to rent out your room, Pet.
I don't fucking understand, Mother.
But you will write the letter, Mother!
Soon dear, soon.
I'm Hanna Greally, and I want to go home.

26.

If I made any kind of complaint, I was
moved deeper and deeper into
this ominous old building.
You were treated like an idiot.
The treatment was often
meted out in smirks
and nods and gasps.
A withholding of a new blouse that
was dropped in for you by Noreen the nice neigbour.
A withholding of information that would benefit you.

A withholding of common decency.
A withholding of any trace of grace or understanding.
A withholding of withholding.
A ham-fisted attempt at sarcasm.
Hanna can't sleep –
well let's move her into the east wing
where she'll have some bedlam buddies.
Hanna is tired of the sewing room –
oh, excuse me, Hanna,
I hear you are tired of the sewing room.
Big guffaws from those ignorant bitches,
their blotchy faces,
their untouched cunts.


27.

When Mother died I knew I was mother-fucked.
Who would claim me out now?
Nothing much happened for years.
Then suddenly I was an orphan.
The house I grew up in was sold.
No insurance was the song on the wind.
Get some rest Hanna, there's a good girl.
When she was alive what had I?
This place. Now what have I? This place.
Yes, I'm grieving. I'm grieving for myself and
that nineteen-year-old girl
who was promised the sun, moon
and a big bowl of glucose.

28.

For the time I was here I had written
thousands of letters.
Noreen's twins made their first holy communion,
their confirmation, and they had a lovely double wedding,
fair play to them.
Noreen didn't write as often as she used to, after
Mother died. I think she was afraid I'd ask her to
claim me out. God knows I asked everyone else.
You were everyone's buddy
until there was a chance you might be asked
for the loan of an address.


29.

Here in the left-luggage department
the time passes out the dust particles
and the dust particles win.
The force of inertia, the tease of tumbleweed.
They interlock like a double genitive.
All that possession and emptiness fills your days.
You come to inhabit terms like
remnant road, rubbish avenue,
abyss with no bliss or put another way
abyssless-bliss, thank you miss.
It's not that we are all lost –
most of us were never found.
We were never lost, we were left.
It's not a lost and loster department,
it's a leave them to rot department.
Find me. I'm Hanna Greally
and I want to go home.

## 30.

One dance sticks out in my mind.
We were well turned out. The excitement
was indescribable. Our chakras were shining.
*Who was that guy you were dancing with, Hanna?*
That was carrot-head from the carpentry shop.
Goretti was brazen and you couldn't muzzle her.
*Did you feel carrot-head's carrot Hanna,*
*when ye were dancing so close?*
Goretti wash your mouth out with soap.
He was going to be a priest.
*Then he met you Hanna —*
*Goddess of the lipstick tube.*
*Goddess of the high heels.*
*Goddess of the suspender bender.*
*Goddess of the nylon knickers.*
We could only laugh, and later I could only sob,
big blubbering sobs that took my breath away.
Men to the left, women to the right.
Desire went in the big noisy grey bin
and dreams of getting out went in there too.

31.

If I ever get a box room
I will cherish it.
I will learn the address by heart.
Lake Drive Box room
or Sandy Cove Drive.
Oh, I'd come down a peg or two.
Mother often said, I'd need to get off
my high horse.
To be honest after nearly 20 years in here
I'd settle for any address,
Sleazeball Alley, Identity Crisis Avenue,
Carpal Tunnel Dr., Witch Road.
I'd have labels made, hundreds of them.
I put them on the backs of envelopes.
Lost Soul Avenue. Lost Soul Drive.

III.

# *Poems Before Covid*

# Homage

The Miss Bonner brought the milk
in a sturdy can with a proper lid.
The journey wasn't a long one,
still she cycled up that hill
and ceremonies had to be upheld.

We were told to make the Miss Bonner tea
and give her bread and jam,
and don't rush her.
If her headscarf slides to the floor
place it round the back of her chair.
Ask her if she needs to use
the outside lav, and if she accepts
don't make a big deal out of it.

We watched her while she drank her tea.
She was fond of the sugar, two please, loveen.
She liked a nice clump of jam on her bread too.
Blackberry if the berries were picked in early October.
She feared the Puca's piss and spit,
otherwise any jam would do.
I might use the outside lav
it still looks a bit narrow —
eye of a needle, loveen, eye of a needle.

When our mother came home —
the pin of our pinafores.
Did ye invite the Miss Bonner in?
Did ye make her tea?
Did ye give her two thick slices of brown bread?
Did ye tell her when the blackberries were picked?

Did ye wear yere manners well?
Did ye wrap her ever-sliding headscarf
around the back of her chair?
Did anyone make rude noises with their plastic sandals
while she was swallowing her tea?
Did ye offer her the use of the outside lav?

# Scullery

A place of cold comfort,
a pot and pan place,
a place to wash potatoes in that spaceship pot.
A place for Andrews Liver Salts,
a treacle tin for rusty nails.
Old oil-stained rags in a ball.

No water came from the taps in the scullery
but from a barrel outside.
One day we will have running water
and when that day comes
women will dance on Jupiter and
we will be liberated
from our picayune half-selves.

A place to hide the Jeyes Fluid
but nothing could hide its smell.
A three-legged stool stood in the corner,
it was brought in for the rosary.
No one wanted to be caught with it.
It had no luck, that stool,
it took nobody's weight.
Although we were only floating feathers,
it still creaked out in agony.

The scullery was there,
and it was name-checked often.
It had the measure of us
or at least our half-measure.
A place of no comfort,
a cold place for Liver Salts,
a puncture repair kit had squatter's rights.
The scullery, a place to be cold in.
A room as empty as our chiselled hearts.

On winter nights the wind howled
round the gable end,
and walloped the scullery door
nearly taking it off its hinges.
A shout rang out,
it snapped our torpor in two.
Close the scullery door
and keep in the heat,
for the love and honour of Christ.

# The Spark

I detest that spark that
flew out of the fire
and burned my mother's leg.
She cried out in agony.
A language we could barely interpret.

Some of us could barely walk.
We didn't know how to help
the one who always helped us.

I think of that day now,
over fifty years later.
I'm lying by a pool in Lanzarote.
I can't say for sure
what sparked that memory.
I can say for certain –
it cut to the bone.

# Mimic

It was no fugue state
but some irascible demon took hold
when the kitchen lino was going down.
He kicked it in temper and created a sinkhole –
the tape and lino-knife in freefall
as he cursed that uneven floor.
We stood like right galoots –
sentinels of sorrow.
'Now look what ye made me do.'

Having lost all their Trojan swagger
the brothers were falling over each other.
Fearing the raised voice
far more than the nose-diving lino-knife –
we scuttled into the back room,
like Burglar Hermit Crabs.
Diddle diddle dee, diddle diddle dom.

A Trojan has-been jumped up on Olympus.
He could take the lino-kicker off to a tee –
we burst in laughing,
we burst out skitting,
our sides were splitting,
the mimicking immortal,
the tail spin complete.
When he embellished the act
with a gomey walk and a slip-sliding face,
we laughed so much that we cried.

# Sanctus

In the front pew sat a row of burly men.
They had big hands, suave as wedding-dress satin.
Save for one burly who had calluses.
They say he worked on the Sistine Chapel
but it was an in-joke for something else,
like the local crib or the cathouse he built.

Sorry for your troubles the echo went,
it doubled and trebled,
the same incantation was everlasting,
sorry for, sorry for
your troubles, your troubles.
A hug from the mother,
thanks for coming loveen.
Not at all. He'll be sorely missed.
The mother was a slight woman barely there –
light as a cupcake.
Her daughter – other end of the pew –
another cupcake.
I know you are,  the mother said, the daughter said.
The burly men had scalded eyes, men from Mars.

The gone brother was also burly.
When he was here he was overheard saying,
in the post office,
I'm sick to the back teeth of this life, without a wife.
He actually had no back teeth
but that's neither here nor there.
He was fond of the Peggy's Leg.
When he was a nipper,
he'd eat them all day if he could.

He was overheard saying the 'back teeth' line
by Lou Lou McLoudmouth,
the biggest gossip in the estate.
Locals say she made it up
just to be in the picture.
People say quare stuff at funerals.

The owners of five sets of scalded eyes
huddled together. Mars bars.
A cupcake at one end,
a cupcake at the other end.
Not a Peggy's Leg in sight.
Nothing to see here
but frames and fragments,
sitting in empty street —
one brother down.

# Canis Lupus

In Cumbria,
Ulverston to be faithful.
It was cold,
not the type hot tea would thaw,
the other type.
The lonely side of sinews cold
though you were in an area called Furness.

It was named in the Domesday book –
'Wolf Warrior'.
Stan Laurel came from here,
so did Bill Haley's mother.
A place of suffragettes.
A hearth of a place.
You could imagine winter stews.
A secondhand shop I'd have loved to rummage,
alas the town's half day.
Ulverston was near the epicentre of an earthquake once.
It nearly fell in.

Airport-bound now on an overcrowded train,
*This train is going to Preston,*
a pack got on, they were loud,
their bags were tired.
They had a seat all to themselves.
The elderly stood.
A wolf whistled at his iPhone,
he howled out, *skanky bitch.*
Other Canis Lupus joined in,
*lemme see, lemme see.*

Cold.
Fear too,
not the type
hot tea would muzzle,
the other type:
bone, tendon, ligament.
I didn't make eye contact.
I had Kim Moore's poems.
I didn't look right or left.
I read poem after poem
until the wolves fell silent.

# Reprisal

Like Hitchcock's birds
the shingles
peck at my back.
On a cold day
when I turn around
not a feather in sight.
Only a faint breeze
and a whiff of revenge.

# Tooth and Nail

When Rocinante O'Reilly rocked up
with her polished spurs,
her Jolie Rouge lipstick,
her onyx earrings,
her gecko-shaped broken front tooth,
she was untouchable.
She regretted telling them
about the dream.
She dreamt there was a nail
in her drink, a toenail.
She didn't know who it belonged to
but it wasn't hers.
It lay there
and as she drank
it began to twitch.
It did Samba
and other runaway stuff.
It never did Bunga Bunga.
They said, pay no heed to her,
she was always odd.
Didn't she eat her own placenta?

# Cavities

They were standing on top of the wall
pirouetting between the broken glass and destiny.
Tossers with a death wish,
but that's not what Missus
from number seven called them,
and she was a daily mass-goer.

Then they started walking on cars.
Not as daring as the broken-glass shuffle
but more destructive for the bonnets that buckled
under their fried-bread brains.

Missus from number seven,
who misses nothing, said,
I know them Gobshites
and all belong to *thum*.

Their grandfather, nicknamed the dentist,
couldn't look at an apple
cos he hadn't four teeth to rub together —
was caught coming out of the sacristy
just before the preamble of
the 'Fourteen Holy Helpers' novena
with a clawhammer down his underpants.

We all knew he was using
that clawhammer
to pluck teeth out of his hole.

# Proof

It wasn't all the state's fault —
you played a cameo role.
You stole those apples.
You also took the biscuit,
looking for compensation for your incarceration.
We didn't just grab you off the street
and give you a life of misery;
you are a thief, you actually stole.
I grant you thirty-five years in lock up
might be a tad excessive for stealing an apple or two
but hell you got three squares a day and a cot —
what more could you ask for?

We are here to improve the lives of survivors
of institutional abuse.
We can hear you when you jabber on about it
but we are going to help you.
We can give you stuff, lots of stuff but no money.
We can give you a lovely heater.
Anyone now for the last heater?
We can fix your windows, we really can.

Look at the state of your rotting teeth.
See what your biscuit eating did now?
As a redress board we can slap in a new set
of teeth for you as soon as we make a mould.

Once you give us proof that you were beaten
black and blue by a hose-pipe
wielded by Father Greasy Smile.
Did you take pictures when Father Magillycuddy

reeked of whiskey and hammered
the teeth out of your skull?
That was a perfect opportunity for a picture.
Where was your polaroid then?

We might not be able to give you a full set of teeth
but you probably have no need of a full set.
What would you be eating anyway,
trans fats and fried bread?
This is how we save the country money,
by giving you no money
just stuff, the stuff of dreams.
When we finish with you
your smile will be seen from Uranus.

White, clear and portable,
you might complain that you only have a half set
but the top set will do all the work.
You can grind your troubles
into your bottom jaw.
O.K. there might be a little suffering
but compared to thirty-five years
of our five-star bleakness,
this will be a cakewalk.

We are giving you a coffin never used.
The quicker you occupy it
the better for my staff.
We want to make a real difference to your life.
This state body is like no other for helping
and improving the lives of survivors.

Are you a survivor?
You need to start acting like one.
No, I repeat, we can't give you the bottom set,
you greedy yoke.
This is not twin set Tuesday.
This is top set Monday.
Now don't come at me or my staff
with the back cheek.
You won't be a burden to the people of Ireland
when we are finished with you.
The name of our organisation is
Humilia, Humilyou, Humilation.
Our staff will provide you with stuff
to help with day-to-day living.
All we require is proof.

# Beware the Geegaws

The 'no you cants'
stack up against you.
They are devious enough,
not impish or puckish, more vengeful.
'I'll put you in your place' vibe –
offering you shiny things first.
Go on, have a bauble.
It won't burst your eardrum.
Doodads don't give you trouble.
It will shine just for you.
*Shine on, Shine on Harvest Moon...*
You can swoon it back and forth
in front of your eyes and hypnotise yourself.
Go on take a geegaw, you might get lucky
and get the ho-ho-ho inked on it.
Recall now that time your post office book
and your credit union book
were a safe house – that time is gone, girl.

Yesterday had no visible dogmas
or cat's Melakas, only clones of 'gone-befores'.
Telling you via earworm,
'no you cants', and other negatives and knockatives.
Knock knock, who's there?
Nobody, obviously.

And God help us if you have a disability
and you win that car in the credit union draw.
the quick draw you have been paying into
since the crab fenced with the octopus.

You can't have that car you just won,
because you have a disability.
It's in the rule book.
How would you drive it with your no legs?
It doesn't matter that you won it.
Invisible has no face, silly.
Take a bauble and go back in line.
Look at your shiny trinket.
Look out for the ho-ho-ho and go with it.
It's the value of you, the super value.
Listen to society and listen good.

Back to the guide book, yo!
Note its colour is duck-egg blue
with a faultline border frazzled and jittery.
How do we read disability,
mental or physical?
What we tick in the empty box
is not always what we think in the full box.
Our gavel may not rest on walnut wood,
still we use it oftener than we should.
We were taught by church and state
to leave 'imperfect' at the gate.

# He Fell Through the Cracks

The boy's name was Abel.
At times he was sunny,
oftener he was sad.
He was non-verbal himself –
the voices in his head
like a Greek chorus,
never took a tea break.

He couldn't tell you what they said.
He went around the house
with his hands covering his ears,
trying to block out the hubbub.

His mother cried the day the van came.
They put him in an adult Psych ward.
He shared the ward with four men
who had their own demons.
They never got a weekend pass,
much less a visitor with some smokes.

Abel deteriorated,
his mother told doctors.
A flock of them around his bed.
The white swans of Coole.
What's wrong love, she'd say.
He couldn't tell her what toy he wanted.
His remote-control dinosaur, his Ninja set!

She guessed on and on for a solid week.
Every toy he owned was named, some twice over.
He slid into the quieter rooms in his head.
He didn't cover his ears anymore.

When his file was analysed,
the professionals said,
Abel fell through the cracks.

He went in in a van,
a jalopy of a thing.
He came home in a box,
a pencil case of a thing.

# We Want Change

Change loses its spinal tap,
when you rap it like a bodhrán.
It loses its front bone, its funny bone
when politicians stick it in a sentence.
Change had backbone once, fadó fadó.
The change brigade has octopus's presence,
they claim words and belt them out.
We want change, I want change,
do you want change? We all want change.
How would your change look?
Would it speak to the homeless?
Would it sit beside an elderly patient
on a trolley in any A & E in Ireland?
What would your change do about this traffic?
My change would be nicer dressed than your change.
My change would wear stilettos.
What would your change wear? Speedos maybe!

Would your change take the teeming snow
from the streets of Galway?
The same snow that's on all our legal tender.
It's like Billy Blizzard here, the capital of coke.
What is change anyway?
It's a word we hear at election time.
They say it, we hear it.
It's a six-letter word with no currency
when it's demeaned by overuse, overdose.

Honeyed words you proffer, the silver lining is free.
Giving change a spin, giving change a bad name.
Making a mockery out of change.
I'm change, I'm pleased to meet you.
Will you vote for me?
A vote for me is a vote for change.

# Mortal

*(in memoriam Gay Byrne)*

Yes, he was loved,
adored and cherished.
He was a mortal not a God.
He knew that better than most.
When night times came
and November folded itself around him,
and his slight shoulders.
He had the thoughts of a mortal.
He wondered what was next.

# Oughterard-ery

*These are people who are coming over here from Africa*
*to sponge off the system here in Ireland.*

T.D. NOEL GREALISH

(at a public meeting in Oughterard on 11th September, 2019,
to fight plans to provide a Direct Provision Centre there.)

Yes it's a noun around town,
it stands for keep them down,
way way down.
Vows were taken and given.
We vowed to keep them out,
we vowed and we vowed,
we the ad-hoc committee.
There was no tenderness in the tender process.
We want to be informed of every move
that every mouse and man make in this town.
This is our town we are proud to be proud
and we say it out loud.
Proud to be proud wearing our ad-hoc-jocks.

Ye are not the persecuted Christians
we were half expecting.
Ye are only the economic refugees
coming over from Africa.
Ye lied bare-faced,
we want the persecuted Christians,
ye have mobile phones
and ye look healthy.

We are ad-Hockery
We are Rahoonery
We are Buffoonery
We are Baboonery
We are Blaggard-ery
but most of all
we are Oughterard-ery
and Oughterard says no.

RITA ANN HIGGINS was born in 1955 in Galway, Ireland, where she still lives. Her first five poetry collections were published by Salmon: *Goddess on the Mervue Bus* (1986); *Witch in the Bushes* (1988); *Goddess and Witch* (1990); *Philomena's Revenge* (1992); and *Higher Purchase* (1996), as well as a memoir *Hurting God* (2010). Bloodaxe Books published her next five collections: *Sunny Side Plucked* (1996); *An Awful Racket* (2001); *Throw in the Vowels: New & Selected Poems* in May 2005 to mark her 50th birthday; *Ireland is Changing Mother* (2011), and *Tongulish* (2016). Her plays include: *Face Licker Come Home* (Salmon, 1991); *God of the Hatch Man* (1992), *Colie Lally Doesn't Live in a Bucket* (1993); and *Down All the Roundabouts* (1999). In 2004, she wrote a screenplay entitled *The Big Break*. In 2008 she wrote a play, *The Empty Frame*, inspired by Hanna Greally, and in 2008 a play for radio, *The Plastic Bag*. She has edited: *Out the Clara Road: The Offaly Anthology* (1999); and *Word and Image: a collection of poems from Sunderland Women's Centre and Washington Bridge Centre* (2000). She co-edited *FIZZ: Poetry of resistance and challenge*, an anthology written by young people (2004). She was Galway County's Writer-in-Residence in 1987, Writer-in-Residence at the National University of Ireland, Galway, in 1994–95, and Writer-in-Residence for Offaly County Council in 1998–99. She was Green Honors Professor at Texas Christian University in October 2000. She won the Peadar O'Donnell Award in 1989 and has received several Arts Council of Ireland bursaries. Her collection *Sunny Side Plucked* was a Poetry Book Society Recommendation. She was made an honorary fellow at Hong Kong Baptist University in November 2006. She is a member of Aosdána. *Our Killer City*, a book of essays with poems, appeared from Salmon in 2019. In 2018, she wrote *Straois/The Smirk*, an Irish-language screenplay. In 2020, during the Covid-19 crisis, Rita Ann became the People's Pandemic Poet Laureate for *The Brendan O'Connor Show* on RTE Radio 1.

PHOTOGRAPH: *Andrew Downes*

# salmonpoetry

Cliffs of Moher, County Clare, Ireland

"Like the sea-run Steelhead salmon that
thrashes upstream to its spawning
ground, then instead of dying, returns to
the sea – Salmon Poetry Press brings
precious cargo to both Ireland and
America in the poetry it publishes, then
carries that select work to its readership
against incalculable odds."

TESS GALLAGHER

# The Salmon Bookshop & Literary Centre

### Ennistymon, County Clare, Ireland

Listed in *The Irish Times'* 35 Best Independent Bookshops